THE

APPROACHABLE

DATA

METHOD

A FIVE-STEP PROCESS TO
SQUEEZE VALUE OUT OF DATA

THE APPROACHABLE DATA METHOD

MARYBETH MASKOVAS

ISBN-13: 978-1-966168-16-4
Library of Congress Control Number: 2025906301

Designed by The Book Designers

INDIE BOOKS INTERNATIONAL®, INC.
2511 WOODLANDS WAY
OCEANSIDE, CA 92054
www.indiebooksintl.com

This book is dedicated to the team at Insight Lime Analytics over the four years that the firm provided services. Each analyst/consultant who worked with me (Ben Clarke, Ryan Vivinetto, Michael Cano, Kristen De Lay, to name a few) inspired me to do better as a manager and a trainer, and of course, Kaytlin Ehardt-Aguilar who was with me since almost the beginning.

While I decided to take a different direction than running a consulting firm, all the people who were willing to join me in the crazy journey of a consultancy startup made it possible for me to dream big for The Approachable Data Method and create frameworks that will hopefully set more organizations up for success in data usage.

Thank you for sticking with me, challenging my decisions when they didn't make sense, and being my inspiration.

CONTENTS

PART I

WHY DATA IS A RIDDLE WRAPPED IN A MYSTERY INSIDE AN ENIGMA

WHEN YOU NEED TO CRACK THE DATA CODE

Almost every business owner or leader has a mystery that keeps them up at night, something they worry about in their business.

If they manage to solve this mystery, it will take the business to the next level. Some are kept up by the mystery of attracting enough customers to sustain sales. Others might find that no matter how carefully they examine their profit and loss statements and how strictly they budget, they are less profitable than their goals. They throw hours, employees, and money at the mystery and still can't figure out how to improve it.

There is a solution. In this modern world of running businesses, we all have a glut of data that we can rely on to help us make decisions. Even the humblest start-ups can access countless trends and data points about competitors for free online, and even midsize businesses generate thousands of data points daily. Large businesses have so much data that they don't know how to keep track of it all.

Somewhere, hidden in all that information, is the answer to those business questions that keep you awake at night. The trick is to crack the code— the data code—to push all the unnecessary information aside and identify the pattern within that data that will transform your business.

What does it look like when a business cracks the data code? When a company digs into its data and gets past the supposed enigma of data, it can see amazing growth and innovation—all based on the information it already has. No new tracking, fancy tools, or new databases are required.

CRACKING THE FASHIONISTA DATA CODE

Enter a fashion start-up based out of New York City. Because if you're building a fashion start-up, NYC is a pretty good place to be. The company had an incredibly unique product—vegan boots made of apple leather! Most vegan boots are plastic, a disappointing way to tout sustainability. The business had a clear cause—remain cruelty-free *and* sustainable by using a renewable resource to create high-quality, beautiful boots (they really are beautiful). The company sells primarily online, and the boots have a high price point (about $300 a pair).

The apple-leather fashionistas came to me while I was running Insight Lime Analytics. While they had a beautiful product and were doing OK, they admitted that they didn't understand much about what was happening with their customers. As with many start-ups, they had ambitions for more sales and growth and struggled to get to that next level. Even though they could see sales coming in and had some tracking set up on the website, it wasn't clear what was motivating people to purchase, how the marketing was performing, and the journey customers were going on before they made a purchase.

They needed this information—it was gold to them. If they could understand more about how customers were deciding to make a purchase, their business would be able to place its advertising in the right places and adjust the website to appeal to its ideal customer.

Like many businesses, this boot company used a marketing persona to craft its marketing and branding. The persona was a successful, ambitious woman in her thirties working as a lawyer in NYC. The business was incredibly granular about what this woman did in her free time, the media she consumed, and her personal preferences.

This persona was the basis of all the branding and marketing decisions the company was making. If the company developed a new ad, the persona was sent to the designer. On the surface, this persona sounds like a pretty good guess—someone who is eco-conscious, fashion-aware, and has some budget to throw around. This is how most personas are created—it's a theoretical picture of who the business owner or an external market research firm thinks will buy their products. But what if that guess is wrong?

If you are a brand-focused business operating with personas, you invest a lot of faith and money in that persona being right for your business. Your ads are catered to that persona, and you might even be designing products with them in mind. If you are wrong, you could be driving your business in the wrong direction. If you're right for some of your customers but not all, you might be excluding a group that could be making you more money.

So, this business approached my firm at the time, and we took all the information the team had given us—the persona and their thoughts on what was going wrong and right—and investigated their data's code. We looked at behavioral information on the site, the personas they had designed, and ad performance. Using the Approachable Data Method, we learned quite a bit about what made the vegan leather boot business tick. A few stand-out insights helped them make better decisions for their business moving forward.

The first insight that hit us was about the customer journey. Many businesses these days invest most of their dollars in digital advertising. And while we wish it weren't true, most of these businesses are hyper-focused on last-click attribution. If a customer comes from Google Ads as the last click they did before purchasing, that's where tools like Google Analytics and Google Ads award revenue.

For this business, which was selling a luxury product at a high price point, it took about *twenty-seven* visits to the site from *multiple* marketing sources before somebody made a purchase. Twenty-seven! You can imagine how your marketing success would seem muddy if you were awarding all that activity to the final click that "pushed them over the edge."

This was groundbreaking for the team to understand because they knew they couldn't rely on the return on ad spend from one channel to understand if their marketing was working. There was a more complex journey they had to evaluate as a premium brand, and their website needed to be a vehicle for that journey for every single step. They couldn't just get someone to the site and optimize it just for them to buy now. The website needed to be a luxury experience that allowed for browsing, research, and exploration. This changed how they were thinking about marketing and there was a reckoning that they would have to have a different longer-term strategy.

The second area that stood out during our investigative work was the company's ideal persona versus those who actually visited the website. We looked at the demographics and psychographics of actual purchasers and browsers. There were several distinct groups, one of which was their target audience—yay! The company wasn't completely wrong when targeting professional women in their thirties.

However, many other personas were visiting the site, and some seemed to be struggling. These visitors were coming to the site many times (a clear indicator of interest and engagement) only to convert at a much lower rate than the company's ideal persona. One example that stood out was a not-insignificant group of men engaging heavily. However, they weren't converting quite as well as some of the other groups.

We brought this information to the team. It was clear that there were other personas that they needed to consider on their website besides thirty-something, big-city female attorneys. The realization produced great conversations about how the current site completely catered toward their primary persona.

You could draw many conclusions about this group of men—were these men buying boots as gifts or as high-end fashion accessories for themselves? And usually, when we start to have that theoretical debate with our clients, we say, "I don't know, maybe we should ask 'em." Many businesses forget that customers are very willing to talk to us directly; often, that's exactly what you should be doing.

Calling up a few of these male customers and asking why they buy your products can be more illuminating than days of combing through behavioral data—which is why data can be a riddle sometimes. You might interpret data as the bits and points generated during clicks and purchases, but it goes way beyond that. The qualitative information you get from asking a customer what they like and don't like about your product is also data be a major unlock for you.

Maybe these men had a *Kinky Boots* moment. Or maybe vegan leather boots are the next hot thing to gift your partner—which is interesting to consider when designing a website. The person browsing the website might not be the end user. If that's the case, how do you create a site that gives gift-givers the information they need to get a lovely gift for someone else? Either way, there was a clear possibility for another market for this business to generate revenue from (which is the entire plot of the movie *Kinky Boots* if you haven't watched it).

ALL THE WAYS THE ODDS ARE STACKED AGAINST YOU

The odds may be stacked against us because nearly 85 percent of data projects fail.[1] For many reasons, we have issues executing the data that our companies produce by truckload. Not to bum you out, but let's go through some of the key things that get in the way of data excellence.

The data problems and mysteries that frustrate the business world only keep growing. For every breakthrough we find in our data, it seems like we've created ten issues that make it harder to manage the amount of data we generate.

CONFIDENCE IN DATA

Even if a business has set up comprehensive tracking and has done its financial forecasting, business leaders lack confidence in their own skills and in the data itself.

Unless a company's CEO is a former chief financial officer or chief data officer, a CEO may originate from one or more disciplines typically portrayed as not being "good" at using data. Many other leaders have a similar internal story: they aren't good at using or understanding data. If leadership can't get past this, it's a very hard issue to overcome to have impactful data projects.

Many employees at all levels of organizations feel the same. We get intimidated by the data and may avoid putting figures in our presentations.

THE EXPLOSION OF TOOLS AND METHODS

There is currently an explosion in the data world of tools and methods. Even data experts can't keep up with every single option available.

Due to the number of tools and the diversity of methods, all businesses, even tiny ones, start to gather this collection of flotsam and jetsam when it comes to their data. Someone decided this tool would be great; someone else implemented

Google Analytics, and that's just gathering data that's not being used. And then someone else says, "Hey, we need this other tool, too."

There is so much complexity in marketing and technology stacks when running a business alone is complicated. If you're also selling a physical product, there's so much going on with manufacturing, shipping, and supply chains that add more intricacy to the business. Data makes the business more complex and becomes forgotten, gathering dust in the corner.

WE DON'T UNDERSTAND KPIS AND USE THEM INCORRECTLY

Business professionals are trained to look at the wrong things. When you go to business school, you talk about key performance indicators (KPIs), and they'll touch on how these KPIs are what you should look at. KPIs are critical for your business—choosing the wrong ones can optimize your business right into the ground, and the right ones can motivate teams to achieve above and beyond. The most common sin of KPIs is to have so many KPIs that none of them have meaning to your business.

Some businesses have KPIs instead of focusing on two or four, losing the true meaning of the word "key performance indicator." Beyond that, a KPI is just an indicator, and many of us forget to uncover the truth of the data in a deeper layer. And it's not just one or two numbers. It's the story behind what the information is telling you. Data always tells a story, but a KPI doesn't.

DIGITAL MARKETING'S OBSESSION WITH HYPER-OPTIMIZATION

You should not forget the sin of overoptimization of marketing. Marketers are so driven to show results that a lot of the language and understanding around the true value (and purpose) of marketing has been muddied. Businesses think that every single dollar of marketing should have an equal or greater output of return on investment and that marketing is one hundred percent of how they drive revenue. That's not true. Marketing is part of driving revenue, but it's not the only cause of the revenue your business is producing.

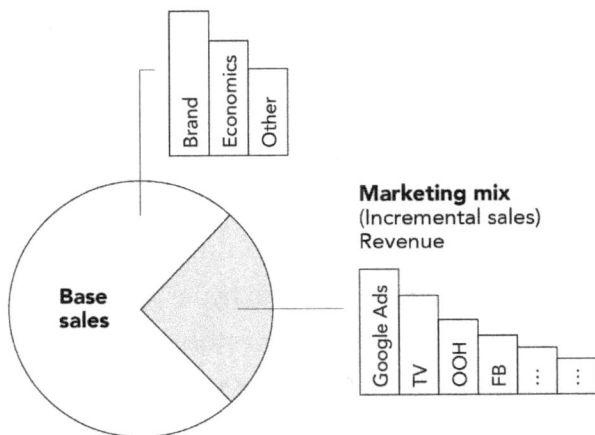

Marketing mix
(Incremental sales)
Revenue

(MMM modeling is a great example of how marketing isn't the 1:1 cause of all your sales. A big portion of sales for brands come from "other" factors like overall brand awareness, which cannot be easily attributed to a single channel or marketing campaign.)

Marketers tend to look at data to confirm that what they're doing is right instead of what the data tells them about the brand and how customers perceive and interact with it. We've forgotten that marketing should be customer-centric, and we've lost our way in obsessing over return on ad spending, spurred on by a channel that wants us to buy more and more ad volume from them and not its competitor.

In a similar vein, within the buying journey of customers, many brands are overly focused on the last mile. There are people in organizations whose titles now are "conversion rate optimization expert." There are conversion rate optimization teams, and they are trying to hyper-optimize this tiny, tiny section of the bigger story of what a customer comes to you for. Should you be hyper-optimizing the final purchase or the customer's total journey? That's a conversation for another day, but this focus on the final mile does mean many businesses aren't focusing resources on the bigger picture that could drive more revenue.

Due to the explosion of conversion rate optimization, we perceive data professionals and our data similarly. We expect data professionals to focus on the final mile, the tiny things. Optimizing a conversion rate can have significant gains if you get a 5 percent improvement in conversion rate, but it's tough to achieve even a 1-percent improvement. If data professionals looked more holistically at the business or website experience, many opportunities would be easier to reach and drive more revenue. For example, if you can solve the issue of a high rate of customers leaving from landing pages, you can increase the total volume of customers going through your whole funnel, which can lead to much more revenue output (faster) than going for the limited gains of conversion rate improvements.

OUR DATA SUCKS

Now for one of the truths that causes the most paralysis in using data. Digital and business data isn't that good. It's so inaccurate compared to data that we look at in the hard science world that it would likely give a scientist a bellyache if we told them what we were basing million- or billion-dollar decisions on. We cannot precisely count the users who come to our site. We cannot always precisely attribute with a 95 percent confidence interval that our website experiment won. Flaws in tracking put data into the wrong buckets, miscount things, and cause discrepancies between platforms that add to the noise.

Our imperfect data creates a weird dichotomy: a business must always chase improved data quality while simultaneously accepting that it will always be bad.

Digital analytics data faces new villains that will continue to eat at data quality. For example, new privacy laws can make it impossible to collect everything you want. As of 2024, there is a war on third-party cookies, with many browsers deprecating the beloved advertiser's cookie. As a result, you get an even less complete picture of who is coming to your site.

When you look at data beyond just your digital analytics, the website you're looking at combines sources with varying degrees of quality. Some data points might be precise, like a count of products and inventory, while others are managed as an individual spreadsheet that one person uploads daily or weekly. You're trying to combine those data sources to create a picture.

Because of this, we spend too much time improving the data and almost no time analyzing and understanding it. Your teams look at your data and say, "Oh, well, the discrepancy between digital analytics and our finance backend is 10 percent, so how could we ever trust this data? I guess we won't do anything with it." So, you spend all this money implementing and then do nothing with it.

WE HAVE NO CONTEXT SKILLS

In Western businesses, we are segmented thinkers. We lack individuals who can identify context and think holistically. In our organizations, this problem makes it difficult to find value in data. This issue is present in almost any department: finance, business analysis, or digital marketing. Many analysts fall into the trap of being a "reporting squirrel," which is not my term but comes from Avinash Kaushik.[2] Essentially, reporting squirrels run reports that nobody reads, and that's their whole job.

Instead, our analysts (and you) should aspire to drive more value for the business. A genuinely excellent analyst with a cross-disciplinary understanding of the business can ask, "Why are you asking this? What do you want to get out of it?" The analyst can dig deeper to help a business stakeholder get the answer they truly want.

Someone good at asking context questions can guide business stakeholders and themselves to the "right" question that needs to be answered and then find that answer.

You could have solved all the other issues in this section, but you're still out of luck without people understanding the context. There's no replacement for having curious people who care about the bigger picture of the business and can interpret data within the context of the company. Artificial intelligence (AI) can't take the place of somebody good at asking for context. It's never going to happen.

You might finish this chapter and think there

are too many problems with insufficient solutions. You may even want to throw your whole data collection engine into the trash. But don't fret. There is hope. Businesses *can* significantly improve outcomes using their data.

3

CUTTING THROUGH THE POLITICS OF DATA

While you may have opened this book to find some easy unlocks about data, there's an unfortunate truth about business, especially data. The truth is that you can only successfully improve your organization's data storytelling and data usage if you are involved in politics.

No one likes that truth. People may grumble, "I don't want to mess with that political stuff." We often think about office politics and remember some colleague we hated who stole credit from their team and sent catty emails. But politics is not always a bad word, and being a good data politician isn't a bad thing.

Every business has different opinions and agendas across departments. The bigger the company gets, the more opinions and agendas there are.

We will talk about how to be a good person and ensure that you're serving the business in what you're doing, not necessarily how to be a manipulative politician. Politics do matter, and here's why.

THE BAD VERSUS THE GOOD

A bad political player wants to harm your data efforts (intentionally or unintentionally). It only takes one person in the company with poor intentions to completely shift the company's attitudes about data—one who speaks very loudly and consistently along the lines of, "We can't trust the quality of the data in this company. I don't know where that report came from." That one person who discounts whatever information is brought and has no challenger will only keep a company working on gut feeling. It only takes one person doing it consistently without a voice of reason to show the other perspective for the virus to spread.

Fortunately, a good data political player can win out against the bad. A good political player promotes themselves and their team, using data to support arguments. The good data political player is respectful and helpful while playing the company political game. They show how data can improve decision-making and help a company grow.

The good wins because a bad political player relies on uncertainty to keep their position. If the game of a bad political player who is anti-data is to question the data every time, sow doubt, and talk about gut feelings, their strategy will start to lose out when a good data player is there and prepared. It's easy to refute "I've never seen that number before—can we trust your sources?" when you've done your homework.

Common Statements	How To Refute Them
"I've never seen that number before. Can we trust your sources?"	Actually, yes, you can trust this data. We have done data audits of all our systems, and I have data dictionaries and discrepancy one-sheets I can show you. The governance team and leadership have agreed that X data source is acceptable to use for this analysis.

Common Statements	How To Refute Them
"I've heard that our data quality is bad."	We have audited our data and decided these data sources are of a quality level acceptable to use. All digital data has some flaws, and we know its caveats. I'd love to walk you through all the data we have if you have time and show you our current data quality status.
"This other approach is better; the CMO likes it more, and X consulting firm agrees."	Thanks for the information. Could you provide the deck the consulting firm used to reach those conclusions? Our approach here uses our internal data sources and current performance to determine the best courses of action.
"How do we know that your analysis doesn't have bias?"	We have a team of professionals with X credentials who did this analysis. We used business context and our expertise to make these recommendations. We intend to improve the business.
"We've spent so much time/effort/money into this project, and there's no way it didn't pay off!"	The data we have here shows the performance of the campaigns with solid measurement. Here are some ways we can optimize in the future based on the data; we have some great opportunities here, and now we know what doesn't work as well.
"That metric looks high/low."	The data I'm showing you is from our source of truth system, and I can show you how it has changed over time.

A good leader clearly understands the KPIs on which their team is measured. You have tremendous power if you can show whether your efforts have improved the metrics or what caused them not to grow and are comfortable justifying your next steps. Leaders who tie their efforts to the business goals can sway leadership and your team to move in a direction that will improve the business.

If you can show that the website's conversion rate hasn't been improving because you need to drive more quality traffic to the site and explain your plan to do so, you can pivot the conversation to the metrics and efforts that will make a difference for the business at that time.

(It's important to note that you should focus on being transparent with your data storytelling. Cherry-picking insights that make your department look good is another bad-player-ism. The solution for cherry-pickers is to focus on telling both sides of the story and to challenge yourself and your analyst team to understand the macro picture so you aren't led astray by what you hope the data will tell you.)

On the other hand, your bad political player is out of luck if leadership starts to look for the understanding behind the good and the bad of their performance. If leadership begins to expect clear suggestions about the next moves and builds trust with you—the good political player—because you're showing them both the good and the bad, the bad political player suddenly has less power.

Original comic by John Kieckner

You might think your experience as a good data player will look like this illustration. Yes, it can sometimes be scary being one of the first to suggest ideas based on the data, and sometimes you can get backlash, especially from those bad political players. Your suggestions can help transform a company from struggling to growing, so it's worth the risk if you care about driving the business's bottom line.

To see how it can be reframed positively, we will go back to the 1960s and David Ogilvy, the founder of the Ogilvy advertising company.[3]

The agency was doing a campaign for tourism in Scotland. Mr. Big, who's paying the bills, says, "We should feature fly fishing for salmon because that is so great, and it's famous."

Ogilvy says, "I agree. It's great. In our survey with your potential guests, fly fishing finished number forty-four in the ranking of favorite activities; maybe we should feature something in the top five."

Sometimes, the person with the data can win the day. Your suggestion based on the data can save your company from spending money in a direction your customers won't like.

WHY YOU HAVE TO
PLAY THE GAME

In brief, you must play the game to protect your team and drive the business's bottom line.

Politics, unfortunately, matter for another reason. If your departments of analytics, data engineering, and finance (insert other technical departments here) aren't playing the game, they can get cut out of the equation. If they aren't advocating for their successes and using data to back up their suggestions for success, they can get drowned out by more vocal areas of the company.

If the data teams don't advocate for data use in the business, don't involve themselves in the board of directors' meetings, assist with data storytelling, and engage in uncomfortable, sticky conversations, they can slowly become irrelevant. Instead of participating in big brainstorming and strategic thinking, they can be there only to provide useless reporting. They become just task doers and not thinkers in the business.

Eventually, they will be cut out of the equation to a point where you're not improving the data quality, you're not using data at all, and those teams start to be viewed as an expense instead of a value-added for a business. If you've seen data teams' budgets being cut, I can almost guarantee that a political battle has been lost—because data is critical to all modern businesses.

ALSO, TO PROTECT THE COMPANY

Data governance is another reason we all must play the political game, even if we don't want to. While it might not seem immediately apparent, governance is an inherently political and strategic conversation for businesses. Governance is how you manage the information you're gathering as a business, how it can be used, and how it can be used against you.

There are many changes in the world of data privacy, which will not be limited to when this book is published. Companies are getting sued for how they use information about their customers. That can be avoided or mitigated by companies creating solid governance at a broad leadership level by discussing and arguing these topics to position the company strategically in a way that supports its best interests—from company growth to protection from litigation. And that conversation is very political.

The legal team will have a strong opinion and make suggestions that could contradict some of the teams' efforts, such as sales and marketing. Marketing, sales, and growth teams must align their agenda with investors and shareholders to grow the business and reckon with the legal team's recommendations. The risks and benefits should be balanced thoughtfully. One team having too much sway can expose the company to more risk or decrease its ability to grow revenue.

Then, what all the teams agree upon must be clearly communicated throughout the organization and followed carefully. It needs to be campaigned, publicized (internally), and championed by leadership. I could go way more in-depth, and if you're curious about the politics of governance, I have a two-part series of blogs about it on my website.

https://www.insightlimeanalytics.com/blog/ground-rules-for-data-pt1

https://www.insightlimeanalytics.com/blog/data-governance-ground-rules-p2

4

HOW TO PLAY THE GAME

Communicating the data is a key part of the game.

One of the toughest parts about data is that it's often hard to communicate. Stereotypically, data experts aren't always perceived as being good communicators. And many non-data expert leaders don't feel as confident on the data side, so they avoid using the numbers for fear of looking stupid or not knowing what they're talking about. It becomes much easier to digest if you break data down into the core pillars of what needs to be understood.

DATA QUALITY

To understand data, you must have a solid communication base about its quality. Be clear about why the data quality is where it is, what goes into maintaining it, and why you and the rest of the company have agreed that the data is in a place where you can trust it. Clear communications across the company about your data quality will shut down comments about being unable to trust the data.

Some tools that help you along the way include:

- A data dictionary—documents that include the definitions of metrics and their sources
- Discrepancy one-sheets—one-page documents that show the current percent discrepancies and any other pitfalls of your different data sources. A common one would be a comparison of revenue in your digital analytics tool compared to the finance back-end data

DATA STORYTELLING

The next part of communicating data is data storytelling. Data storytelling is about effectively explaining the mystery underneath all the information: it's the magic of what it's telling us tied to the business context, woven together by someone who can explain that all tangibly. Someone who can effectively engage in data storytelling can make connections that no one else is making and show the possibilities to others. You *must* be an excellent communicator to do that.

While it's an older movie, any data buff should watch *Margin Call* with Jeremy Irons.[4] In the film, analysts present data to the company's president (played by Irons). He says, "Speak as you might to a young child...or a golden retriever. It wasn't brains that got me here, I can assure you that." While not many company presidents would like to be referred to as a young child or a loving family pet, the analyst who can explain their deep, multi-page analysis in a way that a CEO can understand will change the company's future. Or at least allow the CEO to change the company's future based on their recommendations.

THE APPROACHABLE DATA METHOD

The approachable data method is my proprietary process to cut through the mud of business to find the insights that matter for businesses. The method helps break down the often-opaque discipline of using data to inform business decisions into steps that help improve data outputs for business users and analysts. Using a methodology like this can ensure that resources for data keep flowing into your organization and that you're truly using the data you collect to make a positive difference for your customers (and the business).

DETERMINE THE BUSINESS STRATEGY

The method starts by determining the broader business strategy: Stepping away from the numbers and determining what needs to be accomplished. Do you need to find a way to break into a new market to reach the growth numbers the board has mandated? Have you noticed that you have too many returns but can't figure out why? When data investigation starts with the strategy and business need, it will already steer in a much better direction than many analyses.

Start with what the business needs to accomplish to help make the invisible visible. You know exactly where to start digging to identify hidden patterns in the data. Much like a detective would in your favorite crime/procedural TV show, you get an "aha moment" because you know exactly what you're trying to solve for (personally, my favorite procedural shows are *Supernatural*[5] or *Bones*[6], but I'm a bit of a non-traditionalist that way).

If you recall our vegan boot company from earlier in the book, they made our job easier by coming to us with a business problem. That doesn't always happen, but it is how you need to approach using data. They needed to sell more boots and understand their marketing better to make it easier on the small business, since advertising is expensive. Starting with that picture in mind, when they began to uncover the insights in the data, many business opportunities came up beyond "make marketing better," and my company's analysis was focused on exactly the right place.

The next step in the approachable data method is to uncover opportunities and "losers." As you explore the company's performance, you will identify places where the company is losing money and opportunities to grow revenue. You gather these losers and opportunities in a list.

Not every opportunity is worth acting on. Laying all your options out on the table is where strategic magic happens. You can make decisions with more information than simply gut feeling, often making decisions that will help pivot the company in the future instead of being purely reactive.

FINDING THE OPPORTUNITIES AND THE RISKS

Aside from making it easier to "choose your own adventure" for what to focus on and adjust in your business, the opportunities and risks you highlight can help you think critically about where they might be repeated themes in your business. For example, if you overspend on advertising in one area that isn't leading to a good impact, you could overspend in other categories. Catching something like this will help you understand that next layer—we have overspending in a few areas, and the drag on the business is because you're missing organizational structures. The overspending is the symptom. This allows you to systematically improve the business instead of fixing just one area.

Now that you've fully cracked the code, you can capitalize on the learning using your business prowess. The overspending villain has been identified, and now you can approach the problem with whatever will fix it—perhaps better KPIs and measurement of spending categories across the whole organization. So, with one simple analysis that starts with a business problem instead of "let's throw money at data science," you can systematically improve your business, bringing a lot more uplift than adjusting something smaller.

This approachable data process can be repeated over and over, helping you get the big picture, dig deep, and then zoom out even bigger than before to make major changes in a company. The process works for both small businesses and Fortune 500s. Sure, the scale of the analysis, the deep dive, and the zoom-out at the end will be different, but the impact can be measurable for any business.

HOW IT ALL BEGAN FOR ME

The year is 2019, and there is something rotten in the state of data—the place: Copenhagen,

Denmark. Years earlier, I graduated college with an evolutionary biology and ecology degree. I was then recruited into the world of marketing analytics. It sounds like an odd leap, but the company knew about data science becoming popular in marketing and liked that I knew statistics well. I had intended to model the populations of things like bats, not look at CPAs (cost per acquisition) and CACs (customer acquisition cost), but here we are. The journey took me from Boulder, Colorado, where I started my career, to Copenhagen, Denmark to pursue an international career.

At this point, I had been working in Europe for about six years with companies such as the travel website KAYAK (first, at the smaller Nordic competitor called momondo). Being ambitious, I left KAYAK to become the marketing director for a small mobile game company, then fell into the world of consulting again with one of Denmark's top-voted information technology (IT) firms.

During that time, I was enjoying myself. I had a good life there, loved riding the train to work, and tolerated the rotten weather. But there was something else rotten in the state of data that I could not stop sniffing. Were we really using data to its full potential? I had seen some very satisfying projects that turned around and fell flat on their faces when they were ready to be applied to the broader organization. I also saw that data had a lot of hype and not a lot of practical application at the many companies I had touched in my career. Being ambitious, I decided I needed to tackle this problem independently and that it was time to go home (not just because of the data, but because I was tired of living in a wet sponge and missed the mountains).

I moved back to Colorado in April 2020, mid-pandemic, with just some theories about where I might go next and my mom's attic suite to live in (it's a pretty nice attic, by the way). I started looking for a job, excited to apply my experience with the "more advanced" European companies to an American company. I quickly found what I was looking for (or so I thought). To my dismay, the company's culture wasn't a fit, and the role wasn't as advertised. There I was, frustrated, quarantined, and still no closer to solving my dissatisfaction with how modern companies use data.

I decided that it was time for me to get outside help. I began shopping for a career coach. After a few misses, I found Alicia Marie, the founder of People Biz, from Austin, Texas. After having had one test-drive coach tell me that I had an addictive personality and that I should enjoy my rotten role at a rotten company, Alicia came as a fresh breath of straight-shooter air. On our very first call, after I had filled out an application form and we had been chatting for only a few minutes, she said something that surprised me. She said:

"You need to start your own business."

She thought I was a raw, pure entrepreneur, and I had been spending my career terrorizing all these big organizations as an employee and not owning my own company (OK, maybe my words, not hers). I argued. The world was in shambles. I had been locked in my mom's house, avoiding the outside world for months, and my husband, new to the US, needed a job in cybersecurity. We didn't have a safety net, and no one knew what the world would look like in the next few days, let alone long enough for me to start a business. Plus, I was a great employee. I have driven record results for almost every company I have worked at; I am great in-house.

True to her nature, which I would learn

incredibly well, she pushed back. She said I was ready for this and asked, "What kind of firm would you start?" She wouldn't let it go until I at least entertained the idea.

I said I already had a few on-the-side clients and would start a solo practice. My clients were incredibly happy and gave me a decent amount of money to kick-start myself. I could pick my hours, consult how I wanted, and ensure I wasn't doing any useless reporting or analysis that didn't get used.

"You're not thinking big enough," she said. "This is bigger. You're bigger than that. So, you don't want to be a solopreneur. You don't want to be a one-woman band or be one of those 80 percent of businesses that fail in the first three years. What do you want?"

Once again, surprised but refreshed by her willingness to drive me to bigger things, I said, "If I have a business, I want it to thrive. I want a team of at least five to work for well-known brands and to have a well-regarded reputation. I want to revolutionize the world of data analytics and solve whatever is a mystery. But I don't know if I can pull that off."

And Alicia Marie said, "Yes, you can, but it's not going to be easy, and I'm going to help you every step of the way."

I started pursuing the dream, and Alicia Marie was right. It was not going to be easy. I had the misfortune of starting a business at the worst possible time and place: April 2020 during the pandemic, in the historic little tourist town of Durango, Colorado, which is a three-hour drive to Albuquerque, New Mexico, and a seven-hour drive to Denver, Colorado. It's beautiful but not exactly what you'd call the crossroads of the world for the Fortune 1000. However, the world of Zoom became our ally because nobody was traveling anywhere to have meetings. Everything was on Zoom, so I could meet anywhere. And that little town of Durango turned out to be a home-field advantage when, eventually, travel lightened up, and people would see us and the beauty of south-west Colorado. That's how Insight Lime Analytics, my data strategy consultancy, was born.

Soon, our company shocked many when we started landing clients like Wendy's corporate. We beat out one of the big five firms to get the business and continued to beat them for projects they had been pitching to the company for long before we arrived. We were the little underdog firm that could. It was truly a David versus Goliath story. And when David started racking up success after success, teammates began to join the firm. While ultimately, I decided to stop running a consulting firm to give The Approachable Data method more room to breathe, the firm ended with a 90 NPS score and an 80 percent client repeat rate from the start all the way to the end of the four-year tenure.

The reason for the firm's success was the methodologies that we followed. We were obsessed with finding the true impact and making data usable. There are plenty of easier ways to cash in on data work (implementations, reporting, you name it), but we had a vision.

Along the way, I've learned so much. And now, I've formalized the approachable data method, my proprietary process. The process works so well that I've decided to share it with the world in this book.

In Part II, the five steps of the approachable data method will be examined in detail. Let's explore each step further.

PART II

THE APPROACHABLE DATA METHOD

DETERMINE THE BROADER
BUSINESS STRATEGY

The first step of the approachable data method is to determine the broader business strategy.

Determining the broader business strategy is critical. I have approached data projects throughout my career. Essentially, the concept is this: any investigation or project should be tied to the business's broader short-term, near-term, and long-term goals instead of focusing on only one core area or simply fulfilling an "order" to complete some data task for the business.

Considering what most analytics firms and individual analysts do, this approach can sound surprising. You might say, "All I want is for you to migrate me from Universal Analytics to GA4." (Sorry to everyone who is reading this book years later and has a trauma flashback to GA4 migrations.) I dig deeper, even for something as "straightforward" as a migration. I ask why they plan on migrating, what their broader business goals are for the upcoming year, and what some challenges they've been having around using their data.

The whole purpose of asking these questions is that often, in large corporations, there are efforts in the company that are wandering off the path of the overall business purpose. Each department has its set places they are going, and sometimes, the tie-in to the overall business strategy gets lost as you get further down the corporate ladder. When looking for opportunities in a business or starting a new project, thinking about how this improves the company is an often overlooked step. Is this project really going to drive revenue or other efficiencies? Or did it get created because it would look good on some director's resume?

The goal of determining purpose is also to make sure that whatever investment you put into discovery, the data, and uncovering the right places to look for the answers. You could go into almost any area and discover something worth improving in the business. This is like improving your personal health. If you aren't focused on the big picture, you could choose to buy some supplement that is supposed to enhance your energy while still sleeping three hours a night and smoking a pack a day. The tiny improvement of a vitamin won't outweigh the big-picture things you're doing that hurt your health.

An excellent example of this concept is a past client of Insight Lime, who ran a SaaS (software as a service) business. Like all the stories in this book, it's true, but the names and details have been changed.

This client, let's call him Melvin, wanted to launch a new product service line. The new product would give the tool's power users new features the company believed they wanted. The company needed to figure out exactly how it would price this new segment of its business, what features it wanted to develop in what order, and which ones would make sense to develop at all.

My team could have just started with a simple feature prioritization survey, sent it to their existing customers, and given them the results, and that would be that. Instead, when they first came to us, my team asked questions about what the overall goals were for the business, what he wanted to achieve with this new product, what his goals were for the business as a whole in the upcoming years, and what were some of the issues that were coming up in conversation across the teams that were responsible for developing this new product. After listening to his information and story, the team discovered much more than what the customers wanted.

Because of the type of tool it was, some features would've been much more challenging to create than others. There would be more legal implications, development time, and difficulty to execute throughout the process. On the other hand, certain things about the pricing mattered, and others didn't. He wanted to get certain amounts of profitability from this product. So, it didn't matter what the customer wished regarding pricing. The company had to adhere to some minimums. There were also other goals regarding how that would tie into the pricing of the different products that he needed to consider, as well as the overall strategy if this was going to be a premium product with a subscription.

My team approached this project with that

whole consideration in mind. That output meant that when the study was designed, the team considered this broader business strategy and how questions were asked. The study was created using an external and internal audience to validate some questions.

When the team presented it to him, instead of saying, "Here's the ordered list of the features that your customers would like most and least," the conversation went to a broader, more impactful topic. This was, "These are the features that customers have rated in the survey. However, when looking at this list of development difficulties, there are some good conversations to be had about the order in which things are developed." Tying into this broader business strategy added more value to that initial study and ensured that the direction was correct for that business.

How to determine the broader business strategy (TLDR version):

- Ask questions like a coach about the business goals (open-ended questions about the business goals and fears)
- Review information about where the business is going, including current

overall performance and what has been stated as overall business goals

- Look beyond an individual department
- Determine current pain points and areas of consideration
- Take learnings and tie them back to the broader business strategy

6

MAKE THE INVISIBLE VISIBLE

Making the invisible visible sounds fancy, but it is essentially an approach to analysis that focuses on playing detective and making connections among data sources, interactions, and teams. It's a broader picture than just looking at one data source, creating a table, and making some insights. It's looking at all the threads that contribute to that data, such as the people behind the data points and the context of the situation. It's the "holistic medicine" version of analysis. You're looking at the bigger picture of the why, and methodically examining the potential causes of that why to identify what might have been hiding in plain sight.

You are looking at the business question that needs to be answered first rather than at the data sources in front of you. Imagine it as your "murder board" from a procedural crime show. It would help if you threw some things up that caught your eye, but you're not quite sure how they're connected—yet.

For example, imagine that you're looking into the customer service department of an eCommerce business. You've received customer complaints, and leadership told you, "Fix it or else." You're not sure exactly what's going on there, but you have problems with customer complaints going through the rough, reduced return-purchase rates and increased product returns.

PayPal has a brilliant example of using investigative analysis to make the invisible visible to solve their $100 million churn problem. The business strategy identified in our first step is "we lose a ton of money to merchants who leave." Then, the business brought in a physicist, Ben Ramsden, and his intern to dig into the problem.

The team investigated the biggest issue of revenue churn. They crossed any smaller issues off the list, such as seasonal merchants (Halloween costumes) and bad players who had been kicked off the platform. They identified the top accounts churning and had Ben's intern dig deep into the issue. The intern dug into every system possible —customer service logs and risk compliance to create a list of twenty killer scenarios that caused churn. They set up a system to send the results to customer service, who would call the customers and fix the problems. Ben and his intern made the invisible (the twenty killers for those top accounts) visible so PayPal could do something about it.

The key to this is keeping that business focus in mind, which keeps you from doing an analysis that won't help answer the broader business question, such as for a high return rate at a retail business, "All right, we're just going to analyze customer sentiment on Google and a few other sources." Rather, you will say, "What is causing this issue? What are all the data sources available to me? And what is the story here of what's going on?"

You may look at things like the sentiment scores within written platforms. But you'll also look at call times with customer service representatives. You're going to interview the customer service reps and look at the broader structure of the team. You're going to examine other KPIs that they're optimizing. You may even pull reports of the returned items to look for patterns.

During this process, you will begin to piece together connections among these different areas and follow the threads. This helps you logically find what might have been hidden at the start of your investigation. Often, the issue isn't something you could have fixed by analyzing only the quantitative data points. If the real issue is that the customer service team doesn't have enough breaks, making it hard for them to focus, or you don't have enough reps, you might not see that invisible "killer" of your performance if you only looked at customer sentiment. An issue like that probably has multiple causes, and you might come to the wrong or a less impactful solution by following a traditional pattern for analysis.

Suppose you look at this from the surface level. In that case, someone may think, "Well, we need better customer service representatives." However, when you uncover the next layer, something else may be causing those pain points within the business or an opportunity you could not see before.

Applications to making the invisible visible are:

- Stay true to the business strategy (don't forget!)
- Outline the data sources available to you, quantitative and qualitative
- Keep track of interesting threads
- Tie strings among possible connections
- Dig deeper where there are strong connections to explore the true purpose and source
- Loop your findings back to the original cause and consider the meaning for the broader business strategy

UNCOVER OPPORTUNITIES
AND LOSERS

You might have started off wanting to solve a low conversion rate, and suddenly, you're faced with something like, "Our product needs to be improved." This might give the less-business-inclined people a headache, but it's an exciting time if you're obsessed with growth and improvement. You suddenly have more options for driving the business forward that weren't apparent before.

When you analyze using this method, you uncover business opportunities and losers (or risks). Opportunities include identifying an untapped market or product or something else that can be turned around to add more growth to the business in revenue or brand recognition or whatever the goals of that business may be. Always reference section one and tie it back to the broader business strategy.

There are also losers, which could drag the business down: things that are losing the company money or are at risk for potential loss. And then there's a gray area between whether something is an opportunity or a loser. But essentially, you are taking those opportunities and losers and quantifying them. You can take a look and do back-of-the-envelope math on top of the analysis that's already been done and say, "Okay, well, if we took this process that's broken and takes us six months to do each time, and we were able to do it in two months, then by looking at the number of orders that we'd be able to add by shortening that time frame, we could be earning an additional $5 million a year!"

You can uncover that opportunity and quantify it for your team, which makes it incredibly tangible and actionable. Even if that math isn't perfect, it gets the concept across. You want to think about this opportunity because it's one thing to have an interesting insight and say, "Did you know that our business has these five areas of focus and clients only like two of them?" But if you don't have something that's an opportunity on top of that, then it's not necessarily as actionable. This is what defines the difference between an insight and an opportunity. Insights are fine—you hear them talked about much in business data. An opportunity is better than fine; it's great, spectacular, and exciting.

To illustrate this concept, I'll talk about a client who came to my firm and had worked with us before at a previous business. Two of the employees from this business decided to start an online car insurance aggregator. They were well-versed in the insurance industry; they wanted to be in this popular digital area. They were confident they had a good business model and had some investment they were putting into it. They came in with a lot of excitement and modeled their dreams and ambitions in some forecasting of their own.

They approached Insight Lime and said, "We have these goals, we have this investment, and in the first year, we want to make money and pay ourselves. We want to make marketing investments, which is how much we think we'll get and how long we think we can go. And we think we'll be able to turn around from being invested to bootstrapping in this amount of time."

My team took them through the approachable data method process. As they discussed their goals, we noticed they had lofty expectations for their new start-up. My team was skeptical that there would be enough money for them to pay themselves and market in this competitive industry where digital advertising was their primary driver. So, what the team did was qualitative forecasting, where a look was taken at the bidding—the actual bids for the keywords that would be most impactful for them on Google Ads—and then also looked at the organic growth of competitors in their industry and made estimations of how much those businesses likely invested in search engine optimization. A model was made that showed high, medium, and low investment in these areas and tied into the original projections that they were making. This is a bit more advanced than the back-of-the-napkin math, but it follows the same idea. You need to add a number to the opportunities or losers you find.

This case was a combination of an opportunity and loser because my team came back to them and said, "Actually, you'll run out of money in three months, and you won't be able to pay yourselves, and it's doubtful that you're going to be able to grow this business as quickly as you were expecting. Instead, we recommend starting with an organic first strategy. And we expect you'll need a new investment within the business in nine to ten months."

Essentially, we were saying, "You should keep your day jobs," which no one wants to hear. However, what could be done with this methodology was to uncover what opportunities were or were not there for that business and help them make more informed decisions about what they were going to do moving forward. Wouldn't you rather know that before going down that path rather than at the end of those first three months when you're eating ramen and refreshing your web metrics every fifteen minutes, hoping for a sale?

That story is a cautionary tale. An equal number or more opportunities come out of this type of analysis than cautionary tales or discovery of issues within a business that need to be fixed. A great example is while working at the travel aggregator website momondo; my job was to uncover growth and optimize for the US and

Canadian markets. Canada had been a smaller market for the business for some time. Using the approachable data methodology—before it was named—I uncovered huge traffic and revenue spikes from one source. I investigated and discovered a blogger in Canada who had built an algorithm to quickly identify cheap flights. Then, he would send out those deals to his followers and send them to our websites.

The traffic was huge and legitimate. I spent many days of my job sending information to the sales team to slap the wrists of naughty OTAs (online travel agencies) sending us bad traffic. This blogger was generating measurable growth for us in Canada.

However, momondo had no way to encourage a continuance of this behavior from this guy. If he saw fit, he could easily have shared similar flights through another online aggregator. I saw this as an opportunity to have a referral or influencer program. This was before the whole term "influencers" was a thing. The opportunity here was that he could be encouraged to do this more frequently, incentivizing it for him and continuing to grow more traffic and increase our reputation in Canada as one of the best places to find cheap flights. This was both an opportunity and a risk, as we could lose the revenue to someone else, and we had the opportunity to grow it even more.

What we needed to do next, which is where it links into the broader business issues, was to create a more specialized affiliate program. I presented the risks and opportunities with some forecasts and got the ball rolling on a program that helped contribute to the growth of the US and Canada's revenue for the brand by 120 percent in a year.

Here's the application process from this chapter summarized:

- Look at the visible that you have uncovered.
- Create your "back-of-the-envelope" math (theoretical forecasting) to map losers and opportunities.
- Illustrate the opportunity to stakeholders.
- Have strategic discussions about the options.
- Act on options or advise leaders to act on the available options.

8

LINK FINDINGS TO BROADER BUSINESS ISSUES

Finding one opportunity or area to optimize your business provides only a one-time lift for revenue or improvement. What makes the approachable data method incredibly valuable is the ability to take that specific opportunity and understand what it means for the broader business. There is almost always something underneath this original opportunity or loser you've uncovered in the data linked to something bigger. It's not just that one data point. If you have a customer service issue, it may be linked to an organizational or cultural issue in the company, which you need to solve to outperform long-term compared to your competitors.

What has been rewarded or ignored in your organization that allowed a loser to appear?

Answering this question might not seem like the typical job of an analyst or even a data-minded business leader in another area, but sticking your nose into the business of the rest of the business is how you can find those big changes that can transform a company "from good to great."[7]

To illustrate this concept, let's introduce the next client from Insight Lime. A rocket ship success, a new client came to us who was a sports performance supplement brand (electrolytes, post-training recovery) niched into intense endurance sports like long-distance ultra marathoners, cyclists, and mountain bikers.

My team ran our "Opportunities Analysis" project with them, which is the approachable data method from start to finish across the entire business, not just one focus area. The team looks at everything from their P&Ls to the flow at the warehouse in person. We found over $4 million in opportunities and risks for this brand.

What made the project transformative for them wasn't just the list of opportunities and risks; the link to the broader business issues helped them determine their focus as a leadership team for the upcoming year. My team saw a common thread—the business wanted to keep growing and kept running into pinch points all over the place, from inventory issues to customer service not getting wholesale orders set up in time.

When my team sat down with all the opportunities and losers and looked at the broad business goals the company had given us, the hidden connection was seen. Which in their case was process. They had a process documentation and adoption problem, and that problem was happening with the warehouse staff, the customer service team, and even the leadership team. There was a lot of risk of team members leaving and the knowledge leaving with them, and it took a long time to train new team members, even for basic tasks in the warehouse.

The company went on to map standard operating procedures across every department, which paid off almost immediately when a key member of the marketing team and the customer service team left. The processes saved them countless hours and painful mistakes with the team members' daily work.

Those of you who are skeptics have probably already been thinking this, but it's worth mentioning that sticking your nose into the broader business doesn't always go so smoothly. Sometimes, people don't want to hear your truth, and there will be major pushback as you try to show your excitement for the opportunity.

Our challenge is never to be someone who can't handle the truth. If you're committed to being data-informed and improving the business, set your ego aside and be open to what other departments have to say.

An example of a not-so-happy ending was with one of our clients a few years ago. It was a higher-end bedsheet company that primarily sold online. The company was worried about a drop in its conversion rate over the previous few months. Its internal analysts couldn't find what was going wrong. The company's leadership was starting to get quite antsy about it, and the marketing director was concerned about what he could do to improve the performance of his brand.

My team used my methodology to uncover some interesting things. One was that there wasn't a drop in the conversion rate, at least not in the way they were thinking. The business was looking at the conversion rate on too short of a term. It hadn't looked in prior quarters and hadn't looked at the amount that it was discounting its brand. We found that the conversion rate had been artificially inflated for some time because the company had been aggressively couponing and discounting the brand, which had encouraged more sales at the time.

Then, when the company stopped offering so many discounts, the conversion rate normalized, and the company most likely experienced a sales fatigue effect later. Because it had been encouraging purchases by putting products on sale for so long, it had trained its customers to anticipate a sale. It also had gotten purchases from people who would have made the purchase eventually but just made it sooner.

This coupon frenzy had artificially inflated the conversion rate to a number that wasn't sustainable long-term. This is where the approachable data method starts to unlock some hard truths. The organization was in a pattern of fear, afraid of what it was seeing in the data. It likely had made the original decisions about discounting based on concerns about hitting its targets. It was marketing based on emotions rather than necessarily on the broader business strategy it had set down during the year. It chose to coupon when sales were down instead of looking at the broader "why."

Sales can be down for many reasons, and there is a whole list of ways to improve them that don't involve you immediately reaching for your comfort blanket (or sheet) of coupons. The broader business issue was the company had a bad culture around watching the numbers and a reactionary habit of panicking instead of looking holistically at what it could do to grow the brand. We proposed several things to remedy that, including education: "Here, this is how the conversion rate has been performing. Here are some additional opportunities that you could be focusing on, and here are some considerations about how to have a longer-term strategy for discounting that benefits both your customers and you."

In this case, the business was less than enthusiastic. It wanted a quick fix, and no matter what, it wasn't willing to let go of the quick fix to unlock that systematic change in its business. They didn't ask for our services again. Operating that way as a marketing director or a chief marketing officer isn't a happy way to live out your career—you're always going to be chasing your own tail.

Unless something has changed, I'm sure that business is still operating similarly—which limits the true growth the brand can experience and burns out employees in marketing and sales. It's not a fate I envy, stuck in a loop of reporting on bad results and panicking about it.

The moral of the story is to settle into the discomfort of finding a loser in your business and be neutral about the finding. Use that information to ask questions about how that loser appeared in your business in the first place. The next step is to explore broader systems and cultural concepts within the business that could have caused the opportunity or loser. Following that is brainstorming solutions for that broader business issue that extend into more change, data, and business strategy solutions. Employ outside expertise if you don't have the know-how within some of those areas and want to ask for input. Then, the findings will be presented in a way that educates on the broader business value and encourages action.

CAPITALIZE ON THE DATA

Doing a deep dive analysis, uncovering opportunities and losers, and linking them to the broader business value still doesn't provide long-term change for a business. Capitalizing on the data is the final step that makes this process positively revenue changing.

Capitalizing on the data is building systems and processes that affect positive change around what you have found. There are two layers of systems and processes. The first layer is applying the approachable data method within your business. The second examines the systems and processes that need to be created in the broader business to affect that "how-did-this-happen-in-the-first-place" issue.

Broader systems and processes can improve your organization's knowledge management or change something problematic about your culture. This is where the real magic of data comes from—an analyst or a business leader who can take this extra step and help change the business for the better. This is where data becomes useful on a level that most companies never attain. It's what makes you the Sherlock Holmes or Nancy Drew that every organization is clamoring to work with.

Making long-term change happen isn't as simple as the other steps, but if you have uncovered a compelling enough systematic change, it should be easy to get others excited. Capitalizing on the data is a team effort.

My example in the past chapter is a good example, where clear opportunities and losers were identified and the whole leadership team was engaged in conversation on how to fix it. While it was partially out of our hands as the analysts, my team was there to explain the relative values of different projects and help guide them to the process mapping, which was recommended as the most impactful project.

Another term for this type of project is "operationalizing" the improvement. It's one thing to write processes down for one department and entirely another to make a system and do a company-wide project to improve writing down business processes. This is where you're really capitalizing on your data.

Application bullets are as follows:

- Map the opportunity and the link to the broader business issue and ideate a solution.
- Create a process that can be repeated to solve the broader business issue.
- Create knowledge management to make the process available to everyone who needs it.
- Communicate the process across the organization and execute it continually (operationalize).

PART III

WHAT ARE THE NEXT STEPS?

BUILDING AN APPROACHABLE DATA CULTURE

Like many processes, the approachable data method won't be as effective if you only do it once. Businesses are only transformed when the process is repeated and communicated across the organization and when the approachable data method and good data politics are incorporated. One of the biggest pitfalls in modern organizations regarding data is that they don't use it because they haven't built accessible, approachable methods to make it part of their workflows. Businesses focus too much on tools, tracking, and useless dashboards. Modern organizations need to build a culture of curiosity around the information they already have as a business and how they can use it to be better at their jobs, no matter the department or area of focus in the business.

If you're the evangelizing person initially using the approachable data culture method, you should continue to use the technique in more and more areas of the business and continue communicating it to as many stakeholders as possible.

A business can build enough energy, excitement, and approachability around data so that departments that stereotypically avoid making decisions with data can understand and access what they need through the approachable data method. Talk about data empowerment.

Just as every business needs to be driven by core values, data analytics needs to be driven by core values. As Peter Drucker is reported to have said, "Culture eats strategy for breakfast." Strategy can be more short-term; culture is long-lasting, and what builds culture is core values and then stories and training around those core values. This will require an ongoing culture and become part of the DNA of what's going on in chapter eleven. A key part of that training is what we call "teach data literacy," which will be explored in more detail in the next chapter.

Application bullets are as follows:

- Follow the approachable data method.

- Communicate the results.
- Invite others to collaborate.
- Repeat within different departments to identify opportunities.
- Create your culture of approachable data.

TEACH DATA LITERACY

Writing a book about data without touching on data literacy is hard. While discussing how to teach the approachable data method in the prior chapters, teaching data literacy as an organization is a step you can't skip. Even if you have successfully built a data culture where people are interested in using it, you still need to ensure that you have a company that is not only empowered to use data but also has the skillset required to interpret the information they now have more access to.

Data literacy is about ensuring that everyone in the organization who needs to use data (which in a modern organization is pretty much every single role) can interpret and digest information in a data format. This would include data visualizations like graphs and charts, tables, statistics, and some understanding of underlying data structures. The level of data literacy will vary based on each role's seniority and technical nature.

A data literacy program to bring this to a broader group is incredibly important, especially in the corporate US, because almost every role requires some interpreting data. Especially related to the approachable data model, you must ensure your organization understands that data goes beyond "zeros and ones" and that some of your organization's most valuable data may be qualitative. The approachable data methodology bridges quantitative and qualitative data and examines broader business strategies, processes, and systems.

Application bullets are the following:

- Assess the current literacy in your organization.
- Assess the gaps and identify areas of business that need the most immediate assistance in data literacy.
- Identify partners to help educate, such as the human relations department, external partners, and your internal data team.

- Teach and empower by conducting training and hands-on exercises.
- Build a continual program and maintain systems and processes to identify data literacy growth over time.

INTO THE DATA FUTURE

My vision is that data disciples will evolve into business problem solvers and evangelists, helping modern businesses move forward in a way they haven't been able to before. That's possible today because we can access more data than ever.

When you look into the future of what that looks like, one thing that can be known for certain, no matter when you read this book, is that the amount of data companies gather will keep growing. The approachable data method will never be outdated, no matter how complex datasets become, whether you're evaluating simple financial forecasts or thinking about natural language program processing.

What is also becoming more apparent is that the value of data will keep increasing. With new technologies blooming like AI, the opportunities and threats coming from tools that can grab and aggregate so much mean data is more valuable. AI can also help unlock the approachable data method faster when used correctly. In the data future, approachable data is always going to be relevant, and there will be faster and faster ways to get to the later steps within the methodology and to uncover the hidden.

You will always need someone skilled at uncovering the context, acting as your organization's detective, and helping turn those insights into long-term measurable change. Will it be you?

APPENDIX

ACKNOWLEDGMENTS

I want to thank the entire team at Insight Lime Analytics for their love and support while we wrote this book, especially Kaytlin Ehardt-Aguilar and Ben Clarke, who have stuck with the company through many a roller coaster. Kaytlin, thank you for being the high "C" to my "D" that keeps us thorough, careful, and thoughtful in all our work. Ben, thank you for trusting me as your mentor and trusting the process of going from regular analyst to storytelling superstar.

I'd also like to thank my husband, Vilius. He never reads any of my books, but maybe he will once they're turned into audiobooks. While he isn't a major reader, he is always my rock and ready to hear about my day to the tiniest book-related detail.

Lastly, I would like to thank all my clients, coworkers, and bosses throughout my career.

Without you all taking a chance on me and listening to my wild ideas, I would have never gotten to where I am today. Thank you for letting me dig, ask "What if?" and "What about..." so many times, and for all the other good times we've had together!

ABOUT THE AUTHOR

MaryBeth Maskovas is a data expert living in beautiful, high-elevation Durango, Colorado, with her partner and dogs. Over her career, she has helped major companies and start-ups with innovative ways to use data, including working abroad in Denmark for six years. She founded Insight Lime Analytics in 2020 when she was repatriated to the United States amid COVID-19. Using the consulting firm as the vehicle to develop her Approachable Data Method fully, she officially launched the Approachable Data Method as a knowledge resource in 2025. She closed Insight Lime to reach more businesses with the method of learning resources, workshops, and other services.

RECOMMENDED READING

One of the most valuable ways to learn how to be a more effective data detective is through reading. Many books explain how others, especially data science experts, achieve success. What is learned through reading must then be put into practice.

The books below are some of my absolute favorites, written by experts in leadership, data analysis, and other data-related topics. Pick a book from among these or choose another favorite. But read and act. What you learn from your investment in reading may be the real game changer in your life.

Asplen-Taylor, Simon. *Data and Analytics Strategy for Business: Unlock Data Assets and Increase Innovation with a Results-Driven Data Strategy.* (London: Kogan Page, 2022).

Berinato, Scott. *Good Charts: The HBR Guide to Making Smarter, More Persuasive Data Visualizations*. (Boston: Harvard Business Review Press, 2016).

Clarke, Elizabeth. *Everything Data Analytics: A Beginner's Guide to Data Literacy; Understanding the Processes That Turn Data into Insights*. (Self-published, 2022).

Foreman, John W. *Data Smart: Using Data Science to Transform Information into Insight*. (Hoboken, NJ: Wiley, 2013).

Gutman, Alex J. and Jordan Goldmeier. *Becoming a Data Head: How to Think, Speak, and Understand Data Science,* (Hoboken, NJ: Wiley, 2021).

Kaushik, Avinash, Web Analytics 2.0. (Hoboken, NJ: Wiley, 2009).

Maar, Bernard. *Data Strategy: How to Profit from a World of Big Data, Analytics and Artificial Intelligence*, 2nd ed. (London: Kogan Page, 2022).

Morrow, Jordan. *Be Data Literate: The Data Literacy Skills Everyone Needs to Succeed.* (London: Kogan Page, 2021).

Nussbaumer Knaflic, Cole. *Storytelling with Data: A Data Visualization Guide for Business Professionals.* (Hoboken, NJ: Wiley, 2015).

————. *Storytelling with Data: Let's Practice!* (Hoboken, NJ: Wiley, 2019).

Provost, Foster, and Tom Fawcett. *Data Science for Business: What You Need to Know about Data Mining and Data-Analytic Thinking.* (Sebastopol, CA: O'Reilly Media, 2013).

Reis, Joe and Matt Housley. *Fundamentals of Data Engineering: Plan and Build Robust Data Systems.* (Sebastopol, CA: O'Reilly Media, 2022).

Subramaniam, Mohan. *The Future of Competitive Strategy: Unleashing the Power of Data and Digital Ecosystems.* Cambridge, MA: MIT Press, 2022).

WORKS CITED AND AUTHOR'S NOTES

1   Nick Hotz, "Why Big Data Science & Data Analytics Projects Fail." *Data Science Process Alliance,* April 8, 2024, https://www.data-science-pm.com/project-failures/.

2   Avinash Kaushik, "Six Rules for Creating a Data-Driven Boss!" *Occam's Razor* (blog), October 24, 2007, https://www.kaushik.net/avinash/six-rules-for-creating-a-data-driven-boss/.

3   David Mackenzie Ogilvy CBE (June 23, 1911–July 21, 1999) was a British advertising tycoon, author, and founder of Ogilvy & Mather. He was known as the "Father of Advertising." He was trained at the Gallup research organization, and he attributed the success of his campaigns to meticulous research into consumer

habits. His most notable campaigns include Rolls-Royce, Dove soap, and Hathaway shirts.

4   *Margin Call*, directed by J. C. Chandor (2011, Before the Door Pictures).

5   *Supernatural,* created by Eric Kripke, 2005-2020, produced by Kripke Enterprises.

6   *Bones,* created by Hart Hanson, 2005-2017, produced by Josephson Entertainment, Far Field Productions and 20th Century Fox Television.

7   Jim Collins, *Good to Great: Why Some Companies Make the Leap...And Others Don't* (New York: Harper Collins, 2001).